"Let him kiss me with the kisses of his mouth: for thy love is
better than wine."
Song of Solomon 1:2 KJV

ISBN: 978-0-9763741-7-6

These 4 Lines of Romantic Verse is the concept, creation,
design and ownership of the earpfamilynetwork.org.

WHY YOU SHOULD READ THIS BOOK

Warmly inviting lovers and romantics to lose themselves in the softness and wonder of poetry. Wyatt Woolma Earp's latest book is a unique collection of 100 romantic rhyming expressions, each presenting only four concise and spellbinding lines, along with engaging titles, reflecting on love. Welcoming dreamers and those locked in love's lasting gaze, this collection encourages thoughtful contemplation and gratitude, for the beauty of oneness, memories, the natural world, and the warmth and comfort of affectionate relationships.

We begin with the careful intertwining of nature's imagery, and the subtle moments of intimacy that drive us towards commitment and a shared life experience. Despite the implied density of 100 rhyming expressions, their short lengths make this an exciting, interesting, and heartfelt alternative style, which shines light on the diversity and attention to detail found throughout Wyatt's writing.

From romance and gentle hands, through nostalgia, passion, and journeying, to weddings, dreamlands, God, and space and time as binding – this anthology intricately captures the essence of closeness and lasting connection. Wyatt's writing is relatable and accessible in its clarity, but also deeply human, profound, and powerful, in its representation of what love truly means.

By Rebecca Cullen

Fully Committed

I am fully committed to the cause of love
no matter what the cost may be.
Our bond fits snug as a glove
as it was meant to be.

A Little While Longer

If you wait just a little while longer
you'll see the morning day will bring,
a mutual desire to bond even stronger
though it seems the end of everything.

In Times Past

I didn't know these feelings existed
while we walked together hand in hand.
In times past my love was resisted
but now I sense my horizons will expand.

The Morning Light

We awoke together in the morning light
where I saw that familiar smile upon your face.
I did not want to turn to the left or right
lest I miss the leaning of your embrace.

Single Status

I do remember you in those days
when a single status was my vow.
But long gone are those standoffish ways
and here you stand available now.

The Eyes of God

Stand with me at the window
while the howling wind blows.
But where does the wind go?
The Eyes of God only knows.

White Snowflakes

Let's sit together under a warm blanket
while the white snowflakes fall and sway.
But let's not forget to thank it
for bringing the festive season our way.

The Impact

The impact would be even greater
if she would ever decide to leave.
I would neither resent nor hate her
but only seek secluded shelter to grieve.

Passion Deep Inside Us

.

The warmth of your touch will guide us
into an intimate sacred place.
Oh, the passion deep inside us
will lift us into a slow motion raptured pace.

Irresistible Bliss

I sense your lips are an irresistible bliss
tender and pleasant upon contact.
But all that I would need is just one kiss
to safely seal the trust of our pact.

Don't Be Afraid

Don't be afraid to establish trust
more than what you see in me.
Never be afraid to seek more if you must,
I tell you time will reveal all if need be.

Look Clearly

Look clearly with your radiant eyes
and see a sustainable future or not.
If you cannot see where honesty lies
then love is not love until it hits the spot.

Sense of Duty

There is no sense of duty
that I do all that I do for you.
The quality of being pleasing my beautie
is directly presented to all of you.

In My Dream

Yes, you were in a dream
deep within the recess of my mind.
There you were a precious gleam
like a lost treasure I left behind.

The Beauty Speaks

She thought beauty was my weakness
because I spoke to her with such delight.
Honestly, I should learn to speak less
because her reasoning was all too right!

A Transit Flow

I met her in a transit flow you see
where the crowd was without measure.
She asked if she could sit next to me
and I promptly said: "My pleasure."

A Distant Bell

As we stirred in the darkness

I thought I heard a distant bell.

No, it was nothing more or less

so, I turned back to the sound I knew so well.

Slow Motion

It would be ever graceful in slow motion
if you would extend your reaching hand.
The sacred chamber of my emotion
would beat stronger at your command.

Journey

After 8, let familiar emotions take us
into a sacred place under the moon.
But if we sleep slumber won't wake us
because our journey would end too soon.

Passions

The sun passed beyond my sight
as darkness silently descended.
I tried to resist her passion with all my might
but the draw of her eyes never ended.

Encounter

Oh, she passionately kissed me
upon my waiting neglected lips.
Love was all that I could see
as I melted against her swaying hips.

Women

Women are perfect in their creation,
crafted softly and tenderly in every part.
As they birth forth a human nation
the inclusion of their nature is pure art.

Sit with Me

Sit with me with no space between us,

as close as time will allow.

If human eyes could have seen us

then passion would have rewritten our vow.

Welcome to My Journey Love

Welcome to my journey love
as you promptly prepare to lie back.
If you lay still and look silently above
not one part of you will suffer lack.

My Pleasure

Oh, she laid her head upon my shoulder
because her senses were highly elevated.
But it was my pleasure to hold her
until her evening tide was abated.

The Bed

The bed was freshly made up
where she safely closed her weary eyes.
Don't you dare pull the shade up
lest you cause her conscience to arise.

The Stroke of Midnight

At the stroke of midnight
the clock turns the dark over to the day.
But until we see the morning light
the bed soothes us with an urge to stay.

Our Gathering

This thought came to mind
while taking a stroll down the street.
There is you and no other kind
that makes our bond so sweet.

Winter Weather

Welcome here oh winter weather
in haste to bind us under cover.
The flight of snow falls together
as the door opens to my anxious lover.

The Familiar Sound

The water ran down the ancient creek
but the familiar sound is what drew us.
As we stood hand in hand and cheek to cheek
our hidden spot of grass knew us.

The Wedding Ring

Walk along the path with me
while the birds fly above and sing.
Lift your finger so I can see
that bonded and gleaming wedding ring.

The Train Ride

The train swiftly moves us down the track
while I read and you glance my way.
But there's only one thing that I lack,
the pleasant tone of whatever you say.

My Good Fortune

Why did you let me kiss you
as if you knew I would.
I thought my good fortune through
and discovered no one else could.

I Saw You

I saw you from a distance
stroking your shoulder length hair.
I never knew of your existence
until I took a walk in the morning air.

The Darkness

The darkness is my covering shield
where passions let me feel my way.
But I will not surrender until you yield
and allow my words to motivate you to stay.

The Storm

I heard the wind howl outside my window
while my love slept nestled next to me.
The rain drenched the ground below
as it moved through the coast until three.

My Strategy

I thought of a strategy to delight her
so as to hasten a romantic mood.
As we walked, she held my hand tighter
and led me to descend upon the food.

The Christmas Tree

My wife and I stood hand in hand
admiring our festive Christmas tree.
The Spirit of the Christ took command
and reminded us to love all of humanity.

The Forest Walk

The daylight lit our pathway straight
through the active forest in every space.
The walk together was worth the wait
as we anticipated a cozy fireplace.

Kiss Me

Kiss me softy where it matters most.
The time is plenty at hand.
I give all and more to my precious host
who can elevate me high until I land.

Unfortunate Events

A series of unfortunate events
caused you to turn away.
But if you share until it all makes sense,
I'll listen and learn if you have me to stay.

Excruciating Pain

I never knew the excruciating pain
of gain and then loss.
I was secure when there was gain
but now I must bear my own cross.

The Dream I Dreamt

The dream that I dreamt was as real
as you are standing there right now.
I dreamt that all that you suffer will heal
but only you alone know how.

I Know That Look

Oh, I know that look.

The time to intertwine is at hand.

If you give me a minute, I'll close my book

and then all of me will be at your command.

You are My Weakness

I admit you are my weakness
no matter how much I resist.
I'm drawn to that feminine sweetness
and I'll confess all if you insist.

I Love You More

You say that you love me
but it's true that I love you more.
Did you know whenever you rise above me
I can see all that I adore?

A Sunday Drive

Let's go and take a Sunday drive
where familiarity will not face us.
Take me to where I'll feel alive
and where time will not outpace us.

Are You Mine or His

I hope you are brave enough to say it
because I have a feeling, I know what it is.
At this point, there's no reason to delay it.
Are you going to be mine or his?

You Know Already

Don't make me say it
because I know that you know already.
There's no reason to delay it.
Are we out or going steady?

Do You Remember

Do you remember when we met?
But I didn't really want to meet.
The truth is I'm so glad I let
you sweep me off of my feet.

The Task

I took on the task to find you
by looking and searching here and there.
I was discouraged for a while mind you
but somehow, I knew time wouldn't be fair.

Do You Know

Do you know how to make me feel?

Do you know those tender spots?

Do you know the plan when you kneel?

Do you know how to connect the dots?

My Point of View

I thought I would write several pages
revealing my point of view.
These words will last throughout the ages
because every word is about you.

The Kiss

What did I do to deserve that kiss
and a hug right where we stood.
There would never be a moment I would miss
as I sense your efforts are for my good.

Lake Shore View

This lake shore view takes me back
to the first time I laid eyes on you.
Just think, if I had not left but stayed back
I would have never met you.

Beauty

I've never seen such beauty
where every part is perfectly placed.
Heaven knows if only she knew me
every moment would never be a waste.

I Can Tell

No doubt you are interested in me.

I can tell as soon as you appear.

But that is the way it should be

when love draws two hearts near.

Desire

I don't need to make you want me
or send attention my way.
In your eyes I know what I see
and what you desire to say.

Dilemma

I saw her for the first time
sitting alone in a restaurant after eight.
While I sat mulling over a written rhyme
I wondered if I should approach her or wait.

Our Friendship

I'm not that kind of a person
to uncover all of your privacy.
Our friendship will never worsen
because you'll be alright with me.

Snowflakes

Let's take a walk in the snow
and watch the snowflakes fall down.
We'll see such a wintry show
and blinking festive lights all over town.

Choose

I don't believe what will be will be.

You can choose not to go his way.

If you change your direction towards me

my life and love will be yours today.

Regret

I'll never know for the life of me
why you were not my choice.
I think at the time I could not see
the expression potential of my voice.

The Encounter

Oh, that encounter late last night,

it came upon me so strong.

And afterwards I tried with all my might

to descend down to where I belong.

A Tender Kiss

A tender kiss every now and then
would keep my heart and mind afloat.
If ever you asked me how I've been
feel free to read the entries that I wrote.

Speak Now

If ever there was the right time to speak,
say it now while she's standing there.
Tell her what it is that you seek
because she may be willing to share.

Speak Now II.

Speak now or you'll never know
if romance is in the air.
The time is now if you want to show
that walking together is better as a pair.

Spellbound

It was those eyes that held me
spellbound as if forever.
Oh, how I cherish a sight to see
a vision of us dwelling together.

Valentine

This Valentine will be special to me
since I'm no longer unknown.
Love has made certain for me to see
that I will no longer spend time alone.

Snowfall

Let the snow fall down around us
as we skip along the pathway.
Let's huddle until the evening has found us
content and happy as we lay.

Winter Wonder

Thank you winter wonder for
the season of peace and love.
Christmas is calling us to do more
as the sounds of giving rings in the air above.

Speak Love

Speak to me with a romantic and lyrical tone.

Let your voice convey a kind word.

I find no pleasure in being alone.

Speak love so you can be heard.

Human Lips

A kiss is but a fleeting moment
shared intimately upon the lips.
But the human lips can persuade an opponent
to yield mind, body and swaying hips.

A Romantic Lure

I will yield if you offer a romantic lure,
but it must be crafted to linger long after.
If it's a tender rapture, then I seek no cure
only let the climax manifest through laughter.

A Fleeting Moment

Let this time begin with a hush.

A hand full of words are null and void.

Let the warmth of your breath calm the rush.

Or a fleeting moment we will not avoid.

Time and Space

Let's celebrate intimacy in its purest form
where companions will not find us.
The path we take will not be the norm
where time and space could bind us.

Intimate Verse

I think a book of intimate verse
can impress the mind and the heart.
But you must allow your eyes to immerse
if you want it to flow from the start.

Frustrating

Don't let loneliness block your field of view.

There is always someone waiting.

You can write your own story anew

though sometimes it can be frustrating.

Mysterious

I heard you say you are a gifted lover
and skilled in giving slightly more.
I take the challenge to discover
exactly what you have in store.

Those Hypnotic Eyes

Those hypnotic eyes is what draws you in
and it's futile to try to turn away.
But if by turning you happen to win,
warn others to keep their longing at bay.

These Verses

I've chosen every word with intention
as I write these verses for you.
I see no cause for intervention
because I can see these verses through.

My Life

Let me free you of that thought.

My life is embedded in your own.

Let's savor the connection time has brought.

My whole self belongs to you and you alone.

Gentle Hands

Why don't you take the lead.
I know your hands are gentle to the touch.
If need be, I'll kneel and plead
because I need this so very much.

The Rain Fall

I heard the rain fall against our window
while you slept silently last night.
I laid closer and faced your pillow
and dreamt about you until the morning light.

Dreamland

Late last night an urge possessed me
but sleep kept you bound in slumber land.
I moved closer to see if you would bless me
but the wait drove me into dreamland.

Lovely Toes

There is a sight that you wear well
where the glitter, glamour and polish shows.
If anyone looks down, they can tell
my verse compliments your lovely toes.

The Wedding

It is time for me to lay down beside you.

The wedding has come to an end.

If you are afraid, then let me guide you

since we have a lifetime to spend.

Cheers to Us

Cheers to us and the holiday season.

There is so much to see and do.

We can rejoice together for good reason.

You have me and I have you.

Her Shoulder Length Hair

Oh, the beauty of your shoulder length hair
never ceases to amaze me.
Whenever you lean back in your vanity chair
you are such a wonder to see.

The Christmas Season

The snow has finally fallen down.

The Christmas season is upon us.

The merry hearts of all envelopes the town.

The festive season has won us.

The Fireplace

The fireplace burns warm and bright
as we sit down together side by side.
At the window we see the snow in flight
and hear singing in the sleigh ride.

The Sound of your Voice

The sound of your voice is soothing to me.
I can hear the sweetness in its tone.
Whenever you speak words to me
I promise you you'll never be alone.

Contagious Smile

You always look good to me
especially that contagious smile.
Oh, if only the world could see
what I see beyond your smile.

Good Morning

Good morning my love,
how did you sleep last night?
Did you adore the clouds above
when I took you up in flight?

Love

Love will always overcome hate
because it is embedded in the God above.
If we stay bound in a prayerful state
our faith will be lost in love.

Compliment

Can I compliment you on how you look
through these eyes of mine?
You'd thrill the masses in a fashion book
and delight them so, like fine wine.

Remember

Remember when you danced before me
while I sat in my favorite chair?
Wow! You must really adore me
swaying your shoulder length hair.

Beauty II

This precious beauty is so fine.

I must find a way to win.

But I understand if she's to be mine

I must find a way to begin.

Pursuit

Hi love, can you do me a favor?

I need you to seek her out.

Meanwhile, can you make my heart braver

and remove every shred of doubt?

Bedtime

Tell me when it's the right time
to let everything else go.
Whenever we head to bedtime
I have so much love to show.